THAT'S LIFE
Touching Poems

by
Beryl Butler

To Wendy a Joe.
So nice to meet
you.
From Beryl Butler   x

authorHOUSE™

1663 LIBERTY DRIVE, SUITE 200
BLOOMINGTON, INDIANA 47403
(800) 839-8640
WWW.AUTHORHOUSE.COM

First published by AuthorHouse 12/01/05

ISBN: 1-4208-8729-7 (sc)

Printed in the United States of America
Bloomington, Indiana

This book is printed on acid-free paper.

This book is dedicated to my dear husband David, thank you for your love and devotion. Next I must thank Charlotte for her hard work and excellent illustrations. Also to Mike Forman, who has worked hard from start to finish and urged me to carry on. Thanks to you both.

Beryl

Old Fox

The tired old Fox sat on top of the hill

The hounds were getting closer, eager for the kill.

The field was ablaze with bright red coats

Worn by big fat women and big fat blokes.

The poor Fox had nowhere to go,

So he sat on the hill with his head down low.

Then he heard the sound of a mighty gun,

It was farmer Giles and his eldest son.

One loud bang and then more sounds

The horses bolted and so did the hounds.

"Get off my land!", The farmer said

And all of a sudden they had fled

Over the hills and far away

So the tired old Fox went on his way.

C.A.Thomson

Second Thoughts?

The church was full of people,
The bells were ringing out loud,
The choirboys all stood ready to sing
And outside was a very big crowd.
The groom walked up the aisle,
With the best man just behind,
But there was a great big shock in store,
The bride had changed her mind!

Not Marrying for love?

Edward's asked me to marry him,
He's ninety and terribly rich.
He takes me to all the posh places,
In fact he proposed at the Ritz!
The money is the attraction,
Though he's not got long in this life,
So, if he changes his will in my favour
Then I'll be his good little wife!!

Billy's Wish.

I've written a letter to Santa,
I'm a nine year old lad.
I hope he brings me what I want
Like a home and a mum and dad.
My home is under a railway bridge
In a box is where I lie,
It was freezing cold last night
I prayed that I wanted to die.
My clothes are torn and dirty,
My feet are blue and numb
I can't hold out much longer
I wish I had a mum.
Just a few weeks to go,
I hope that it goes fast
I've got a crust of bread left I hope
That it will last.
So Santa, see what you can do
I'm feeling ill and weak,
Find me a loving home and get me
Off the street.

Time To get Rid?

I've been courting for twenty years or more,
But no sign of any ring.
So it's time to dissolve the partnership,
I'm ending it with Jim!
He smokes just like a chimney
And he's drinking himself to death
And I'm getting fed up with his temper,
Bald head, bad teeth and bad breath!

Fancy Free?

It's time for celebrating,
I'm over my fourth divorce,
But I've gained a big house in the country,
Also a yacht and a racehorse.
Now I'm on the look out
For husband number five,
No more oldies for me,
Just a toy-boy, young and alive!

That Cat!

I wish my cat would sleep all night
She woke me up at three.
I couldn't get back to sleep again,
So I made a pot of tea.
I settled down at four A.M.,
But she woke me again at five,
Now it's time to get   up for work,
I just can't open my eyes.

Pay Back Time!

It was the old tiger's
Last day at the circus.
No more whippings
That were plain to see,
So when the Tiger's trainer came into the cage,
The old Tiger had him for tea!

My Little Pet

There's a fairy in my garden,

I call her Tinkerbell

She sits among the flowers

In the corner by the well.

The first time that I saw her

I was standing by a tree

And as I turned,

There she was, looking up at me.

She stood there for a moment

Then waved her tiny wand

And landed on a lily

In the middle of the pond

I love my little Tinkerbell

I see her everyday

I hope she stays forever

And never goes away.

Little Annie:

It was five a.m. the workhouse,
Annie was doing her chores.
Little cold feet rushing around
On dirty floors.
Her tummy was rumbling loudly
As she went on her way,
if she didn't get done by five p.m.,
She wouldn't get fed that day,
But tomorrow she was leaving
to a whole new way of life.
The grocer's son loved her
And wanted to make her his wife.
Well Annie worked 'till six that day
So she never got fed,
Her little body was tired and weak,
As she climbed into her bed,
But soon it would be morning
And she'd walkout this place for good,
The big doors closing behind her
and into the arms of her love.

A Likely Story!

Dad's had a bad day at the races,
So we've got tell mum a big lie.
Dad said he got mugged
On the way back home,
By a man with a squint in his eye!

Magic?

Morris was a magician,
He could make people disappear,
His wife said
Her mother was coming to stay,
So he prepared
For the grumpy old dear!

Bottoms Up!

It's party time folks at the Uni,
Too much brainwork,
Not enough fun!
So Tom's got the wine and the whisky
And I've got the vodka and rum.

Our Little Love.

We've just said good bye to Tootsie,

Our old dog, who died in her sleep.

Dad buried her in the garden

Under the willow tree by the seat.

Her basket is by the fire side

Her collar and lead by the door.

Everything she ever played with

Lays scattered all over the floor.

Her water bowl is in the kitchen

A bone lays there untouched,

Little footprints all over the lino,

Mum can't bear to wipe them up.

So we've said our goodbyes to Tootsie

And all sat down and had a good weep,

About the little love that's gone out of our lives,

Our Tootsie, who died in her sleep.

Never Again!

Grandma took me shopping,
She sneezed as she got on the bus,
Her teeth went whizzing through the air
I sat embarrassed and blushed.
She said that they felt uneasy
And something was wrong with the plate,
But when she got home she discovered
She'd put Grandad's in by mistake!

Confused?

I went to see my doctor,
He said what can I do? I said is it time to come off the pill?
Now that I was Sixty-two.
He asked how long I took it for,
I said thirty years or more.
So he wrote me another prescription
And showed me to the door.

Old Ned

The old donkey walked the length of the beach,

Big fat children weighing him down.

Now he's enjoying retirement with me,

After paying the man fifteen pounds!

Christmas Eve.

I'm sitting halfway up the stairs
It's Christmas eve, you see.
I'm sitting with my hands in prayer
That Santa remembers me.
He didn't come last Christmas,
Mum said things were a bit tight
I remember sitting up in bed
And crying all that night,
But dad has got a job now
And things are looking good,
We've got a great big turkey
And a big Christmas Pudd.
And there's a large tree in the corner
And a fire in the grate
And a glass of wine for Santa
And a mince pie on a plate.

Busy Hands?

My lovely Easter bonnet
Was huge and round,
With ribbons and pretty laces
And chicks all sewn around.
Bright yellow in colour
That everyone liked.
Poor mum sat making it
All through the night.

Looking Back?

Sally gazed through the mirror,
Some white hairs had appeared
And a few more wrinkles on her brow.
She was getting on in years.
Oh! to be seventeen again
When she was crowned
Miss Clacton on sea,
precious moments remembered,
Never again to see!

Three Cheers For Granddad!

Granddad's gone into an old folks home.

Our home's not the same any more.

I miss the bedtime stories

Of how he helped to win the war.

Barney sits in his basket

No granddad to take him a walk.

Dad's lost his drinking partner

And mum won't even talk.

No-one to have a laugh with

Or share a bit of fun.

We all sit by the fireside

Looking dead bored and glum.

So he's coming back tomorrow

and we'll all be happy again,

He only went in that home yesterday,

But we won't let him go in again!

Blue:

Blue is my favourite colour,
Like blue skies
On a summers day
And the lovely colour of bluebells
That flower in the month of May
And the colour of my darling son's eyes
That light up my everyday.

Just Like Heaven.

The wood was a picture of bluebells
The scene took her breath away,
She was just a young girl from the Convent,
Who sometimes went there to pray.

Not A Good Idea!

I started my diet this morning
I've put on a stone in weight
So I had a banana for breakfast
And for lunch I had a grape
At teatime I had an apple
At supper some lettuce and spam
I can't keep it up any longer,
So I'm staying the way I am.

C.A.Thomson

Sadness and Tears.

I went to school the other day,

My teacher told me to go away.

She said my work was very bad

And wanted to see my mum and dad.

Well I went home and sat and cried

Because three weeks ago mum had died.

There was Tim and me and sister Kate,

I was ten and she was eight.

Our Tim was tall like the trees in the wood

He said he could look after us

No clean clothes, no food to eat,

In mum's apron pocket I found a sweet.

Dad left home, like he once did before,

He couldn't just cope anymore.

Kate is crying, can you hear,

Who will wipe away her tear.

Tim is sitting by the telephone

Praying that our dad will ring home.

I'm trying to do the best I can,

But I'm just a lad, Tim's more of a man.

Dad will come home, but we don't know when,

We just want to be a family again.

APRIL:

Daffodils and Tulips

Dancing in the breeze.

Glorious blossom adorning the trees,

Birds working overtime

Building their nests

April's the month I like best.

Garden Blues?

I do love the weeds in my garden,

It's much prettier than next doors,

I water them every morning

And pick them to go indoors!

Boredom?

Spring cleaning time is here again!

I'm cheesed off before I begin,

There's beer stains on the carpet

And dirt all trodden in.

There's cat hairs on the sofa

And dog hairs on the chair

And cobwebs everywhere I look,

Just hanging there in mid-air.

The curtains look all faded,

The paintwork needs touching up.

Whoops! I've broken a nail,

I think it's time to pack up!

Feeling Proud!

I stood across from the Cenotaph,
My heart almost bursting with pride
And then I spotted Granddad
With his guide dog by his side.
A man in a million was this man
He'd been to hell and back.
He never said much about the war,
But we knew he was shot down by flack.
But now he was proudly marching
With those heroes all around,
Their medals shining in the sun
And red poppies covering the ground.

Pimples!

I've got pimples on my chest
And pimples on my tum,
Pimple on my back
And pimples on my bum.
I've pimples on my face
And pimples in my hair.
Oh my giddy aunt!
I've got pimples everywhere!

Vain or What?

Grandma's hair
Is going white
Granddad's is very grey,
Mums is a lovely auburn colour
Dad' vain,
So he wears a toupee!

Naughty Tiddles

The Goldfish swam around its' bowl all day

Lonely and looking fed up.

The cat thought "what an existance",

So quickly gobbled it up!

C.A.Thomson

Thank You Mum:

The little lady I call Mother
Means everything to me.
She fetched me from the orphanage
When I was only three.
She said I was 'Little Miss Special'
The very best thing in her life.
That was fifty years ago,
She's now at the end of her life.
So, dear lord, when she meets you
In your heaven up above,
Tell her that' 'Little Miss Special',
Thanks her for all her love.

Missed His Chips?

Cecil died on Friday,
His wife wasn't very pleased
She was cooking his favourite dinner
Fish, Chips and mushy peas.
She wished he had waited
And passed away that night,
At least he'd have eaten his dinner
And plum pudding with angel delight!

Small Fry.

Poor little sausage
Being fried in a pan.
Who chose him I ask?
When there's liver, eggs and ham!

In the Money!

We've just bought a castle in Scotland,
Great views and in its own grounds.
My dad has won the Lottery,
Winning 10.2million pounds.
Mum has said what she wants most.
Two gardeners, two cleaners, two cooks.
Dad said all he wanted was
An Au-Pair
Big chested, eighteen, with good looks.
I go to a big posh school now
And I've learnt to speak la- di-da.
I'm driven around by our chauffeur
In our brand new car.

Time to Go.

Sixty five years together,

Now it had to come to an end.

Harry had just buried Lorna

And his heart wouldn't mend.

Her slippers were by the bedside

her gown on the bedroom door.

On her pillow was the smell of perfume

The kind she always wore.

Her glasses lay on the bible

The book she read every night.

Harry laid on her side of the bed

And prayed he would join her that night.

NO Prospects?

I went for a game of bingo
At the local bingo hall.
I rather liked the caller, Oh yes!
He was handsome, clean shaven and tall.
When the bingo was over
At precisely ten o'clock,
He came over and introduced himself
And said he liked me a lot.
He asked me if he could walk me home,
He had a glint in his eye,
I said you're only a bingo caller
And not my sought of guy!

My Little Friends

I'm sitting in my garden
As quiet as I can be.
A hedgehogs just gone rushing by
And a squirrels run down a tree,
A robins in the bird bath,
Wet through and having fun.
Four doves are sitting on the fence,
Enjoying the morning sun.
The thrush is singing his heart out,
A bluetits just gone in its' box
And further up the garden,
There's my friend the poor old fox.

Another Way of Life?

I was born into poverty,
So I know all about being poor.
Seeing the rent man call each week
And hiding behind the door.
No food on the table,
No bed where I can lay,
Just a dirty old mattress
Someone had thrown away.
Searching through the dustbins
For anything to eat,
Feeling ashamed of begging
On the corner of our street.
Body like a bag of bones
Where flesh once used to be.
Maybe I'd be better off dead
No-one will ever miss me.

Driving Him Mad?

I've got my fifth driving instructor,
His name is Valentine Black.
He looked fit and well
When he got in the car,
But soon had a panic attack!
He thought my driving was atrocious,
My emergency stop knocked him out!
So after an hour of driving around
he paid me to let him out !

Silly Man!

Granddad tripped over the Christmas tree,
Now he's got a broken leg.
Grandma found him flat out on the floor,
With fairy lights all round his head!

Santa Came at Christmas?

Santa came on Christmas eve,

I pretended to be asleep.

He reminded me of dad a bit

He was clumsy on his feet.

He fell into my bedroom

And landed on the floor

And said a naughty word,

That my dad had said before.

He came up to my bedside

With presents big and small

And then he tumbled yet again

And fell into the wall.

I did feel sorry for Santa

He did smell of beer a bit

I'll tell my dad in the morning

And see what he makes of it?

Naughty Polly!

I'm looking after the Parson's parrot
And its language makes me blush.
He swears from early in the morning,
And then carries on until dusk!

C.A.Thomson

Back Again:

My Tinkerbell, The Fairy
Has come to see me again.
She was missing for the winter months,
Away from the wind and the rain.
Now everyday I see her
She's as happy as can be
When I'm in the summerhouse
She sits upon my knee,
But her favourite place is the rosebed,
It must be the beautiful smell,
I love her more than anything
My little friend ,Tinkerbell.

Tinkerbell and the Petal.

I was picking roses this morning,
My fairy friend was there.
A rose petal suddenly floated down
And landed in Tinkerbell's hair.
She danced around in amazement,
A wonderful sight to see.
I look for her every morning now
And I hope she looks for me!

Hopalong Doc.

Jake sat in the Jailhouse
brought in by a Miami Cop.
He was driving along the highway
When he had to pull over and stop.
Now he was facing the Sheriff,
a mean man with deep set eyes.
He told Jake he wanted the truth
And not a pack of lies.
He said someone had shot Doc Brady
In his foot and it was mighty sore,
Jake said it wasn't him,
He'd only shot a wild pig and a boar.

Indian Country!

The young cowboy rode through the canyon,
Guns loaded and ready to draw.
Then he saw Big Chief Sitting Bull
With Running Water his Indian Squaw.
The cowboy fancied the lady,
So he winked as he rode by
Big Chief saw what happened,
So he shot the young cowboy
And then watched him die.

Home Sick!

She was a typical English beauty,
Who worked in a burger bar.
A talent scout spotted her
And said she would go far.
She made it big in Hollywood
And was known for her beauty worldwide,
But she missed the English way of life
And its glorious countryside.

What a Loser!

Joe Stood in the Casino

His face white with shock.

He went in with his pockets bulging

And he had gambled away the lot.

The Manager of the Casino

Walked over and said to Joe

You've always been a good customer,

So he gave him one free go.

Soon Joe was back in the money,

With pockets all bulging, the same!

He started to walk towards the door,

Then turned around and went back in again.

Retirement.

I've just become a pensioner
After working for forty odd years.
It was an emotional day for me,
With Handshakes, kind words and cheers.
I've been a bricklayer all my life
And as I packed my tools away,
I remembered the day I first started,
A cold winters day
I was told to get the fire going,
Then make a pot of tea.
I was skinny in those days,
So the brickies poked fun at me,
But soon I was working with Lenny,
A big man built like a tank,
He taught me everything I know,
So it's him I have to thank.

Washday Blues

Grandma and Grandad's not talking

They had a bit of a row.

His white shirt went in the washer

And came out pink somehow.

He shook his fist in temper

I thought he'd never shut up

Well now he's got no shirts at all

Grandma's cut them all up!

C. A. Thomson

Greedy!

Santa, my dad wants a Porsche,
Our Katy wants a rocking horse.
I want a train set and a drum,
Oh! and don't forget our mum.
Grandma wants five hundred fags,
Granddad wants a Porsche like Dads.

Missing something?

Dad said he'd take the dog for a walk,
We told him it died last year!
So he put a collar and lead on the cat,
And walked him along Brighton pier!

A special Love.

We stood in the airport
My lover and I,
It was nearly time
To say our goodbye.
His arms tight around me,
His lips brushing mine.
My tears on his face
And his on mine.
Going to fight in some war far away,
leaving for a year or more.
One last brief kiss
Then away onto the plane
Choking back the tears
And hearts full of pain.

Our Son.

We've just had our first baby,
He's the image of my spouse.
We can't wait to get him back
To our little house.
He looks so cute, so beautiful,
He gives us such a thrill,
Oh how we love him so
And always will.

Young at Heart?

Grandma said she was lonely
And wanted a man in her life.
Mum said the vicar was single
And was looking for a wife.
Dad said he wouldn't want Grandma,
She wasn't much of a catch!
The vicar should look for a dolly bird,
Not a pensioner with a moustache!

Bad Times.

The tramp sat in the market place,
his scruffy cap laid on the ground.
I'd had a good win at the races,
So I gave him twenty five pounds.
I put it in his top pocket,
Where I thought it would be safe
And as he turned to thank me,
I saw his tear stained face.
He reminded me of Granddad
A veteran of the first world war
And as he reached to shake my hand
I gave him twenty pounds more.

Nearly A Gonna?

Kitty is so naughty
She fell into the loo,
I was in the shower at the time
And didn't know what to do?
Little Charlie tried to flush her away,
I told him he mustn't do that.
You do that for some things, Charlie,
But not to Kitty, our little cat!

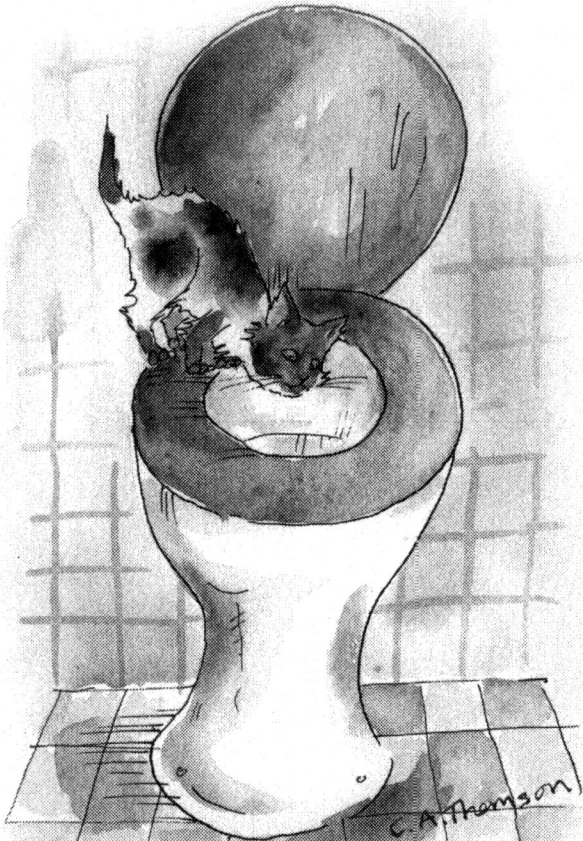

The Climb.

Sue and Bill thought they would climb up the hill,

But halfway up Bill felt very ill.

Sue said,'Stay here while I fetch your mum'

So down the hill she did run.

Now bill's mum was very sad Because Bill was her favourite lad.

She ran to the docs

She knew he was in

She'd just been there to see him

About a boil on her chin.

The doctor came out with his little black bag

And said 'How is the poor lad'.

Sue said it was getting late

And it would be dark by half past eight.

The three of them got into the car,

He drove so slow, it seemed so far

After a while they did arrive,

But poor old Bill had gone and died.

Fed Up with Work?

I've washed the dishes
And done the floor.
I've baked a cake
For Granddad next door.
I've fed the cat and walked the dog,
been round the park for my usual jog.
I've changed the beds, cleaned the brass
I've put out the rubbish
And cut the grass.
I'm so fed up
And I've got a bad head
Blow it all!
I'm going back to bed.

Poor Mary.

Poor Mary sits alone in her flat,

just her and kitty her little black cat.

She's lived there fifty years or more,

All alone and very poor.

She didn't have any family

She would have loved a son,

She would have made someone such a lovely mum,

But her husband died at the age of twenty four

He got shot down during the war.

She remembers the day they said goodbye

It was warm and sunny late in July.

He told her he loved her, that's the last thing he said

And six weeks later she heard he was dead.

With tears in her eyes she turned to the wall,

where his picture hung, he was handsome and tall.

She whispered goodnight, then sat down and cried

And during that night, poor Mary she died.

Little Rascal!

My Dad's bought me a puppy,

I've called him Mister Woo,

But all he ever does each day

Is eat and wet and pooh.

He wet on my Dad's new cashmere coat

And on Mum's favourite hat,

And now he's wet on the parquet floor,

he should not have done that!

C.A.Thomson

Moonstruck?

The moon was shining,
But not all that bright,
He desperately needed a pal.
A twinkling star was very close
And had those thoughts as well.
Soon they edged a bit nearer
The moon shone more brightly
And felt very proud,
But just as they were about to kiss,
They were both swallowed by a cloud!

A Bit of a Snob?

I went to my son's wedding,
She looked lovely and he looked great.
Two hundred and Twenty guests were there
Thank goodness they had a big cake.
I didn't take to the bride's mum
She looked odd and not very glam.
My son said she'd just had a face lift,
But to me, she looked more like a man!

Dad's Hero. Brian Clough.

I would love to be a footballer
And play for dad's favourite club.
It would have been Nottingham Forest,
That's where his hero did good.
Dad talks about the good times
When the lads played with great pride.
Dad tells me about it, often in tears,
I've never seen dad cry before,
But I did on the day Cloughie Died.

Together:

Old Charlie walked through the graveyard,

His body racked with pain.

Holding a bunch of roses

For his darling Mary Maclaine.

When he reached her graveside,

He thought he would sit for a while

And then there appeared an angel,

Who gave him a beautiful smile.

She said all his heartache was over and took him by the hand.

Charlie never said a word,

He knew what she had planned.

In the distance he saw Mary,

His darling Mary Maclaine

And after that night in the graveyard

No-one ever saw Charlie again.

Lightning Source UK Ltd.
Milton Keynes UK
UKOW01f1217100917
308817UK00010B/91/P